DATE DUE

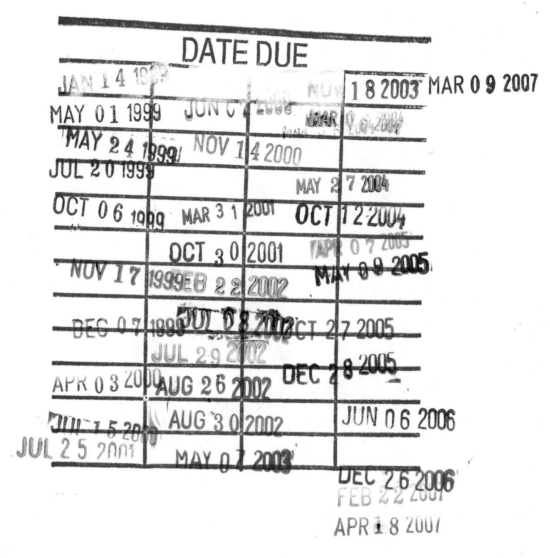

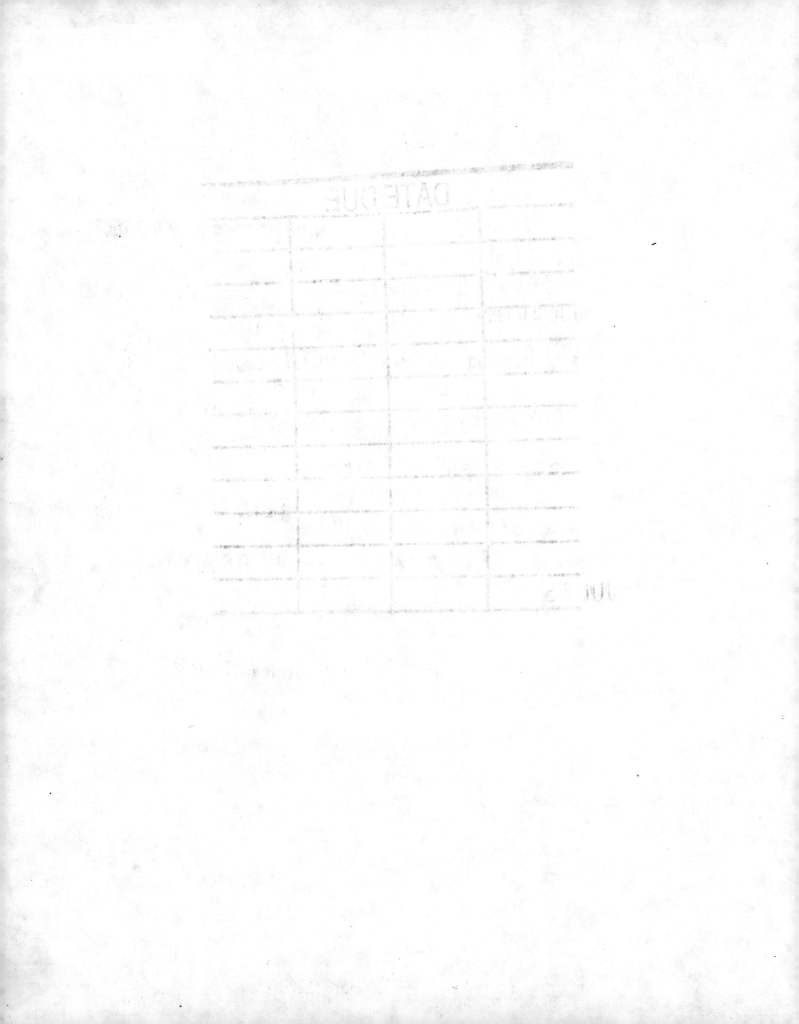

LAUNCH PAD
LIBRARY

WORLD OF THE RAIN FOREST

ROSIE McCORMICK

STAMPLEY

How to use this book

Cross-references
Above some of the chapter titles, you will find a list of other chapters in the book that are related to the topic. Turn to these pages to find out more about each subject.

See for yourself
See-for-yourself bubbles give you the chance to test out some of the ideas in this book. They explain what you will need and what you have to do to see if an idea really works.

Quiz corner
In the quiz corner, you will find a list of questions. The answers to the quiz questions are somewhere in the same chapter. Try to answer all the questions about each subject.

Chatterboxes
Chatterboxes give you interesting facts about other things that are related to the subject.

Glossary
Difficult words are explained in the glossary on page 31. These words are in **bold** type in the book. Look them up in the glossary to find out what they mean.

Index
The index is on page 32. It is a list of important words mentioned in the book, with page numbers next to the entries. If you want to read about a subject, look it up in the index, then turn to the page number given.

Contents

Rain Forests of the World

Rain forests are full of thousands of different kinds of trees and flowers. All of the world's rain forests are near the **equator**, which is an imaginary line around the middle of Earth. It is warm there all year, and it rains every day. There are rain forests in Africa, South America and Asia.

One land
Millions of years ago, all the land on Earth was joined together in one piece called Pangaea. Animals and plants that lived on Pangaea looked alike. But, gradually, Pangaea split into **continents**, and slowly the plants and animals on each continent changed to suit their new **environments**.

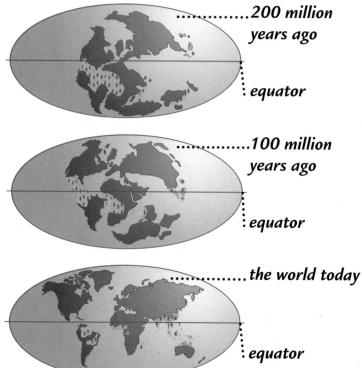

200 million years ago

equator

100 million years ago

equator

the world today

equator

▲ As Pangaea moved apart, it carried rain forests to different parts of the world.

The top layer of a rain forest is called the canopy.

The middle layer is called the understory.

The forest floor is dark and hot. Only a little light reaches the floor.

Some trees tower above the canopy. They are called emergents.

High and low
Animals live in all parts of the rain forest. Some, such as monkeys, spend their lives high up in the tree branches. Others, such as tigers and peccaries, live on the forest floor.

▼ Most rain-forest plants are evergreen, which means their leaves stay green all year round.

Quiz Corner

● In which places do rain forests grow?

● What is the name of the top layer of a rain forest?

● When all the land on Earth was joined together, what was it called?

● What is the middle layer of a rain forest called?

look at: Rain Forests of the World, page 4

Weather and Water

Rain-forest plants play an important part in shaping our weather. They give off water **vapor**, which turns into clouds and falls as rain. Rain-forest plants soak up the rain and the cycle starts again.

3. When the vapor in the clouds has cooled enough, it turns back into water and falls as rain.

2. The vapor rises into the air. It then starts to cool and forms clouds.

1. The sun warms the water in oceans, rivers and plants and turns it into vapor.

All the water on our **planet** is **recycled**. It travels from the land and oceans to the air and back again. This movement of water is called the water cycle.

Flooding

Every year, millions of gallons of rain fall on rain forests. About half of that rain flows into rain-forest rivers. The rest falls on leaves and into the soil. Often, during heavy rains, riverbanks burst and parts of the rain forest flood. Trees help soak up the water and hold the soil together.

▲ This part of the Amazon rain forest in South America has been flooded by heavy rains.

◀ These rain-forest trees in Asia are being cut down and burned to clear the land for farming.

Burning down trees

Each year, rain-forest trees are cut down and burned. When trees are burned, they give off into the air a gas called carbon dioxide. Scientists think that if there is too much carbon dioxide in the air, it will harm the planet by changing our weather.

Quiz Corner

- What is the movement of water from the land and oceans to the air and back again called?
- What often happens to parts of the rain forest during heavy rains?
- Which gas is given off when trees are burned?

look at: Animals of the Amazon, page 10; Rivers and Streams, page 20

The Amazon Rain Forest

The Amazon rain forest in South America is the largest rain forest in the world. It also has the richest plant life, with about 30,000 different kinds of flowers and 4,000 kinds of trees. Like all rain forests, the Amazon has special kinds of plants and animals that do not live anywhere else in the world.

In demand
Mahogany is a **hardwood** tree that takes many years to grow. Every year, lots of mahogany trees are cut down and sent all over the world to be made into furniture. Some people are worried that soon there will not be any mahogany trees left. They want to protect these trees by asking furniture makers to use trees that grow more rapidly.

▲ The Amazon rain forest stretches for thousands of miles and crosses into several countries, including Brazil and Peru.

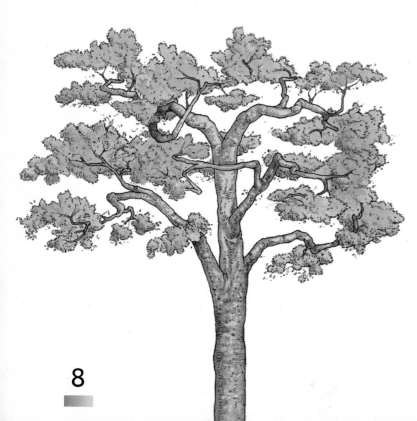

◄ Mahogany trees have long trunks, which can grow to be 80 feet tall before the first limbs branch out.

The tree of life

The muriti palm is a very useful tree. From it come oil and wine. It can be made into timber, cork and fertilizer. Farmers use the fertilizer to help **crops** grow. The muriti can grow to be 80 feet tall. This is as tall as a six-story building.

▼ When it rains, plants called bromeliads fill up with water, and small animals, such as frogs, live in them.

SEE FOR YOURSELF

Use an aquarium to see for yourself how plants grow in a hot, wet place. Place a layer of charcoal and gravel at the bottom of the tank and cover it with compost. Water the compost, then plant ferns and palms. Put a clear cover on top of the tank. Place it in the sun and remember to water it.

Growing on trees

Bromeliads grow all over the Amazon rain forest. They wrap their roots around tree branches to keep themselves in place.

Quiz Corner

● In which rain-forest plants can frogs live?

● Why is the muriti palm important to local people?

● Name a tree that is sometimes cut down and made into furniture.

9

look at: The Amazon Rain Forest, page 8; Rivers and Streams, page 20

Animals of the Amazon

The Amazon rain forest is a noisy place. From the tallest tree to the forest floor, you can hear birds squawking and monkeys howling. There are animals everywhere, including butterflies, beetles and ants. Hundreds of different kinds of **reptiles** and **amphibians** live in the forest, too.

The forest floor
The Amazon forest floor is dark and damp. Few plants grow there because the thick canopy overhead blocks out sunlight, which they need to grow. But lots of animals live on the forest floor, including jaguars, agoutis and peccaries.

The jaguar's patterned coat helps it hide among the trees.

Young jaguars learn to defend themselves by playing and fighting with one another.

Many rain-forest frogs have colorful, poisonous skins to keep other animals from eating them.

Howler monkeys are some of the noisiest animals that live in the Amazon rain forest. The calls they make to each other in the morning can be heard from far away.

The peccary has strong jaws and sharp teeth. It sniffs around the forest floor, looking for roots, nuts and seeds to eat.

Rain-forest birds
More kinds of birds live in the Amazon rain forest than in any other place on Earth. Most live in the canopy.

The agouti lives alone in the forest. It feeds on grass, fruit and roots.

▲ The toucan has an enormous beak, which it uses to pick fruit and insects from the trees.

The chameleon is a reptile. Its long toes grip tree branches.

Quiz Corner

● Why do few plants grow on the rain-forest floor?

● Which animal has a patterned coat to help it hide among the trees?

● What does the agouti eat?

look at: Asian Animals, page 14

Asian Rain Forests

Rain forests stretch across Asia and parts of northern Australia. These rain forests are different from the Amazon rain forest because they do not have such a thick canopy. This means more light reaches the forest floor and many more plants can grow, including trees, flowers and fruits.

▲ Rubber is collected from the rubber tree by stripping off part of the tree's bark. The runny rubber flows into a bucket.

Rubber trees
Rubber trees grow in Asian rain forests. The rubber is collected from the trees and used to make tires, shoe soles and many other things. In the past, rubber trees grew only in South America, but travelers planted young trees in Asia. Today, more rubber trees grow in Asia than anywhere else in the world.

▲ Pitcher plants often grow on the rain-forest floor. They feed on insects, which crawl into the tube-shaped leaves at the bottom of the plant.

SEE FOR YOURSELF

Make a wall chart. On your chart, draw as many things as you can that are made of rubber or have rubber parts.

Fruits of the forest

Asian rain forests are full of different kinds of juicy fruits, such as mangoes, starfruits and lychees. When they are nearly ripe, these fruits are picked and sent all over the world. You may have seen some of them in your local supermarket.

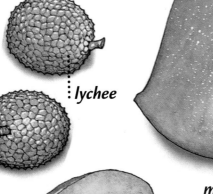

lychee

mango

starfruit

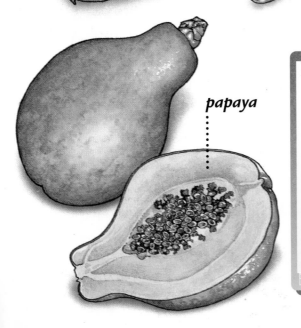

papaya

Plants for weaving

Rattan is a tough and stringy rain-forest plant. Long stems of rattan are used to make mats, hats and chairs.

Quiz Corner

● How is rubber collected from a rubber tree?

● What is the name of the largest and smelliest flower in the world?

● What things can you make from rattan?

look at: Asian Rain Forests, page 12

Asian Animals

An Asian rain forest, like the Amazon rain forest, is home to many different kinds of animals. Thousands of insects crawl over dead leaves and tree branches. Some of these insects are so tiny that you cannot see them, but others are bigger than an adult's hand. Apes, such as orangutans and gibbons, swing through the canopy, while elephants and tigers roam the forest floor.

CHATTERBOX

Asian elephants live in groups, called herds. Each herd can travel over an area up to 800 square miles. That's about the size of a large city.

◀ In Asia, elephants are trained to move heavy logs. They help clear the land for farming.

*The tiger is the biggest kind of cat in the world. It hunts alone, traveling long distances every night looking for **prey**.*

Knocking down trees
In India and Southeast Asia, Asian elephants live on the edges of the rain forests. They have small ears and short tusks. Asian elephants eat leaves, which they pick from the trees with their trunks. When the leaves are too high, the elephants knock over the trees to reach them.

Quiz Corner

- Do Asian elephants have short or long tusks?

- When do tigers hunt?

- Which kind of eagle lives only on a group of islands in Southeast Asia?

The monkey-eating eagle lives only in the Philippines, which is a group of islands in Southeast Asia. It builds its nest in tall trees that poke above the rain-forest canopy.

This snake, called a cobra, is brown to help it blend in with the leaves on the forest floor. This blending is called **camouflage**.

The orangutan spends most of its time in the canopy eating fruit, leaves and plants.

The world's largest stick insect is called the Malaysian wood nymph. It is difficult to spot on the forest floor.

look at: African Animals, page 18

African Rain Forests

Some rain forests grow on the sides of mountains. These rain forests are called cloud forests because clouds often cover the tops of the trees and make them look misty. There are cloud forests scattered across Africa.

Mosses and lichens

In African rain forests, thousands of tiny bright green plants, called mosses, grow just beneath the canopy. They cover tree trunks and roots like a soft carpet. Many animals, such as tiny spiders and mites, live in the mosses. Long plants called lichens, also grow on trees. They hang from the branches and look like cobwebs.

▲ These fungi are growing on the fallen trunk of a rain-forest tree.

◄ Mosses and lichens can cover tree trunks and branches, rocks and stones.

Fungus

Fungi do not have leaves or roots and are not green like plants. They live on plants and soak up food from them. Mushrooms and toadstools are kinds of fungi. Many fungi grow well on or near the rain-forest floor, where it is damp and dark.

Bamboo

Bamboo is a grass that grows in warm, wet places. It is found on the slopes of many African rain forests. Bamboo flowers only once every thirty years. Animals, such as lemurs, eat its stems, leaves and shoots.

▶ The golden bamboo lemur feeds on a type of bamboo that is poisonous to humans and many other animals.

look at: African Rain Forests, page 16

African Animals

In Africa, many rain forests have been cut down, but a few are left in western Africa. The largest of these stretches across the country of Zaire. There, animals such as gorillas and chimpanzees live in the trees and on the forest floor.

All together
Gorillas belong to a group of animals called apes. They live together in families, made up of one adult male, several females and their young. Male gorillas are larger than female gorillas. They have shiny gray fur on their backs and are called silverbacks.

Building a nest
Every night, gorillas build nests in which to sleep. They break off branches and make simple platforms either in the trees or on the ground.

Bedtime
Gorillas spend their days on the forest floor, eating, playing and cleaning each other. They make their nests just before dark. Each adult gorilla builds its own nest. Baby gorillas sleep with their mothers.

▼ Gorillas are vegetarians. They roam the forest floor looking for juicy plant stems, leaves and shoots to eat.

Clever chimpanzees

Chimpanzees also belong to the ape family. Chimpanzees are smart animals. Some have learned how to make and use simple tools. Unlike gorillas, chimpanzees eat meat as well as plants.

▲ Chimpanzees are good at climbing and often rest in trees.

Quiz Corner

- In which country would you find Africa's largest rain forest?
- Where do gorillas sleep?
- Which animals have learned to use simple tools?

look at: Weather and Water, page 6; The Amazon Rain Forest, page 8

Rivers and Streams

Rivers and streams run through every rain forest. The Amazon River runs through the Amazon rain forest. In some places the river is narrow, but in others it is so wide you cannot see the other side.

Flooding the rain forest
Each year, during the rainy season, the Amazon River bursts its banks and floods parts of the rain forest. When this happens, many plants on the shore are covered by water for up to six months of the year.

▲ The Amazon River splits into hundreds of smaller rivers, which twist and wind their way through the rain forest.

The South American river dolphin swims along the Amazon River looking for fish to eat. It has more than 100 sharp teeth in its mouth.

The manatee is the largest animal in the Amazon River. It uses its split top lip to pull up plants from the riverbed to eat.

When the Amazon rain forest is flooded, the water can be very deep. If you wanted to see the forest floor, you would need diving equipment!

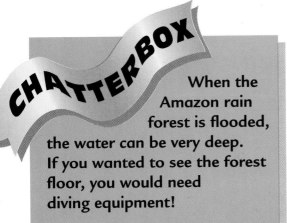

- Which is the largest animal in the Amazon River?

- Which meat-eating fish swim together in large groups?

- How many teeth does the South American river dolphin have?

The caiman belongs to the same family of animals as the alligator. It floats in the water, waiting for prey, which it snaps up in its strong jaws.

Piranhas swim together in large groups. They are meat-eating fish and can tear flesh from the bones of their **prey** in minutes.

look at: Animals of the Amazon, page 10; Asian Animals, page 14

Rain Forests at Night

Rain forests are just as noisy at night as they are in the day. Some animals sleep, but many others wake up. Animals that come out at night are called **nocturnal**. They live in all parts of the rain forest. Many nocturnal animals have large eyes, big ears and good senses of taste and smell. This helps them find food easily in the dark.

The night monkey is the only nocturnal monkey in South America. It lives in the Amazon rain forest.

Night eyes
Most nocturnal animals can see well in the dark. They have large eyes that take in more light than small eyes. The eyes of nocturnal animals sometimes seem to glow in the dark.

The African bush baby eats sugary gum found under the bark of a certain tree. It leaps from tree to tree, using its legs and tail to balance.

Bats

During the day, rain forest bats **roost**, or sleep, together in large groups. They hang upside down from trees with their wings folded across their bodies. At night, the bats wake up to feed. They eat insects, fruit and the sweet juice, or nectar, from flowers.

The world's biggest bat is the Malay fruit bat from Southeast Asia. When its wings are open, it is as wide as a large toy kite.

The tarsier has huge saucer-shaped eyes. It lives only in a few rain forests in Southeast Asia. The tarsier uses its long toes with flattened ends to cling to tree branches.

◄ Many nocturnal animals feed on rain-forest fruits and flowers. They are attracted by the strong smell of rain-forest flowers.

Quiz Corner

- Which name is given to animals that come out at night?
- Where does the largest bat in the world live?
- Why do many nocturnal animals have large eyes?

look at: The Amazon Rain Forest, page 8

Rain-Forest Peoples

Thousands of **peoples** live in rain forests around the world. They can find all they need there. For food, there are plants, fruits and animals. Some peoples grow **crops**, and many know how to use plants to make medicines.

The Yanomami Indians

The Yanomami are the largest group of peoples living in the South American rain forests. Each morning, Yanomami men go hunting with bows and arrows tipped with poison. Often this poison comes from the skin of a certain rain-forest frog. Boys are allowed to hunt with the men from the age of five, but Yanomami women stay at home.

▲ Yanomami men hunt monkeys and other animals with bows and arrows.

All together

All the Yanomami Indians in a village live in one large, round house called a yano. A yano is made from trees bent into a dome shape and then covered with leaves.

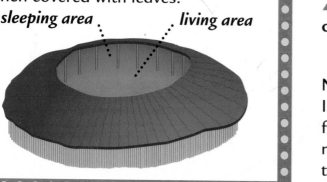

sleeping area *living area*

New neighbors

In the past, only a few peoples lived in rain forests. But in the last 200 years, many more have made their homes there. All these peoples depend on the rain forest for food and shelter.

24

▲ This Yanomami child is wearing sticks and bead necklaces.

Quiz Corner

- In which rain forests do the Yanomami Indians live?

- What is the name of the large house in which Yanomami people live?

- Where do the Yanomami find the poison for their arrows?

look at: Rain-Forest Peoples, page 24

Forest Fruits

Rain forests are one of the richest **resources** on Earth. Some rain-forest plants are used to make medicines, and others are made into foods, such as oil and fruit juice, or eaten just as they are. Each year, hundreds of new plants are discovered, and many of these are useful, too.

Going shopping

Supermarkets all over the world sell hundreds of things from rain forests. Coffee, cocoa, pepper, nuts, bananas, pineapples and avocados all grow in hot, steamy rain forests.

CHATTERBOX

Next time you chew a piece of gum, think about what is in it. Chicle, which comes from sapodilla trees in the Amazon rain forest, is used to make chewing gum.

Cape gooseberries are the fruit of a small plant that grows in South America.

Starfruit grow in Asia.

Ginger is a root that grows in Southeast Asia.

Avocados grow in South America.

Brazil nuts grow on tall trees in South America.

Chocolate is made from cocoa beans, which grow in South America.

Vanilla is the seed-pod of a South American orchid.

Coffee beans grow in Africa and South America.

Some cosmetics are made from rain-forest oils and fruits.

Pineapples are a valuable rain-forest fruit.

Cola is made from the kola nut, which grows in Africa.

Bananas are an important food crop.

Papaya is a sweet fruit.

Peanuts grow in South America and Africa.

Lychees are the fruits of an Asian tree.

Nutmeg is a spice.

Pepper is one of the earliest known spices.

Cinnamon is the dried bark of a Southeast Asian tree.

Cashew nuts grow in Asia and South America.

Lifesavers

Different parts of plants are used to make medicines to treat illnesses such as heart disease and cancer. The rosy periwinkle from Madagascar is used to make a medicine that helps fight a type of cancer called leukemia.

SEE FOR YOURSELF

Make a forest fruits scrapbook. Collect pictures of rain-forest plants, flowers and fruits. Divide your scrapbook into sections for the different rain forests in the world. Tape or glue each picture in the correct section and label it.

Quiz Corner

● Name six things that grow in rain forests.

● In what is chicle used?

● From which country does the rosy periwinkle come?

look at: Rain Forests of the World, page 4

Saving the Forests

Huge areas of rain forest have been cut down to make lumber for building and to clear land for farming. Trees have also been cut down so that gold and silver can be mined. If people continue to destroy rain forests, forests could disappear completely, along with all the plants and animals that live in them.

▶ Today, furniture is often made from **softwood** trees such as pine.

Wood for furniture
People make furniture from softwood, which grows quickly, rather than from slow-growing **hardwood**. This helps make sure there will always be enough trees. In many rain forests, new trees are planted to replace the ones that are cut down.

▲ These enormous trees come from the Amazon rain forest in South America. Workers use saws to cut timber, which is sold all around the world.

Keeping rain forests safe
Some rain forests have been turned into national parks. It is against the law to cut down trees there. National parks help protect all the animals, plants and people that live in the rain forests.

▲ These people in Southeast Asia are planting young eucalyptus trees. Most of the rain forest around them has already been burned down.

Keeping an eye on things

Around the world, special **conservation** groups, including the World Wide Fund for Nature, work hard trying to save rain forests. They tell everyone what is happening to the people, plants and wild animals that live in the rain forests. Find out from your local group what you can do to help.

Quiz Corner

● Why have huge areas of rain forest been cut down?

● Why have some rain forests been turned into national parks?

● How can replanting trees help protect the rain forest?

Amazing facts

☆ Did you know that the leaves of some rain-forest trees never touch or overlap, even though they grow close together? This means that all the leaves get as much sunlight as possible.

● Marmosets live in the Amazon rain forest. They are the only monkeys to drink tree juices. They use their teeth to cut through the tree bark and suck out the liquid.

☆ Hoatzins are birds that cannot fly well. They live in trees around rivers in South American rain forests. Hoatzin chicks escape from their enemies by jumping from the trees into the rivers. When they are safe, they use claws on their wings and feet to climb back up into the trees.

● Some rain-forest plants have enormous leaves. The Victoria water lily of the Amazon River has leaves up to 6 feet across. They are strong enough for a child to stand on.

● Anablepses are amazing fish. They swim near the surface of the Amazon River. Their eyes are divided into two parts, so they can see above and below the water at the same time!

☆ Thorn bugs are insects that live in South American rain forests. They sit mostly on thorny tree branches, sucking out juices from under the bark. Thorn bugs look like thorns, which keeps other animals from eating them.

● Sloths are hairy animals that live in South American rain forests. They spend up to eighteen hours a day hanging from tree branches without moving.

☆ The world's smallest bat is found in the rain forests of Thailand in Southeast Asia. It is called the Kitti's hog-nosed bat and is only about 1.5 inches long. That's about the size of a large bumblebee!

Glossary

amphibian One of a group of animals, such as frogs, that can live both on land and in the water.

camouflage The markings or colors on an animal that help it blend in with its surroundings so that it cannot easily be seen.

conservation Taking care of the planet by protecting its plants, animals and resources.

continent One of the seven big land areas of the world. Earth's continents are Antarctica, North America, South America, Africa, Asia, Europe and Australia.

crops Plants that are grown for food, including wheat, corn and rice.

equator An imaginary line around Earth, halfway between the North and South Poles.

environment The things around an object.

hardwood The wood of some trees, such as mahogany. Hardwood trees take many years to grow.

nocturnal Animals that are active at night.

peoples The different groups of people that live in a country.

planet A large object in space moving around the sun or another star.

prey The creatures that other animals hunt and eat.

recycle To use an object or a material again.

reptile One of a group of cold-blooded animals with skeletons, such as snakes or lizards. The skin of reptiles is usually hard and scaly.

resource Something that is useful or valuable to a person or to a country.

roost A place where birds or bats rest or sleep.

softwood The wood of some trees, such as rubber and pine. Softwood trees grow more quickly than hardwood trees.

vapor Moisture in the air that can sometimes be seen as steam, mist or clouds.

Index

Published in the USA by
C.D. Stampley Enterprises, Inc.,
Charlotte, NC, USA.
Created by Two-Can Publishing Ltd.,
London. English language edition
©Two-Can Publishing Ltd, 1997

Text: Rosie McCormick
Consultant: Cecelia Fitsimons
Watercolor artwork: Stuart Trotter,
Bill Donohoe
Computer artwork: D Oliver,
Mel Pickering
Commissioned photography:
Steve Gorton

Editorial Director: Jane Wilsher
Art Director: Carole Orbell
Production Director: Lorraine Estelle
Project Manager: Eljay Yildirim
Editors: Belinda Webber,
Deborah Kespert
Assistant Editors: Julia Hillyard,
Claire Yude
Co-edition Editor: Leila Peerun
Photo research:
Dipika Palmer-Jenkins

ISBN: 0-915741-79-2

Photographic credits: Biofotos (Brian
Rogers) p12l; Britstock-IFA (Bernd
Ducke) p8; Bruce Coleman p5, p7tr,
p7cl, p11, p29; Colorific! (T. Aramac/
Camara Tres) p28; Steve Gorton
p26, p27; Frank Lane Picture Library
(Phil Ward) p18-19c; NHPA (Nigel J.
Dennis) p19r; Oxford Scientific Films
(Konrad Wothe) p17r; Premaphotos
(Ken Preston–Mafham) p16-17c;
South American Pictures (Tony
Morrison) p20; Still Pictures (Mark
Edwards) p25; Tony Stone Images
front cover; Zefa Pictures p12r, p14,
p24.